DANGEROUS ...OR NOT?

SHARKS
AND OTHER FISH

TRACIE SANTOS

Rourke
Educational Media

A Division of
Carson
Dellosa
Education

Before Reading: *Building Background Knowledge and Vocabulary*

Building background knowledge can help children process new information and build upon what they already know. Before reading a book, it is important to tap into what children already know about the topic. This will help them develop their vocabulary and increase their reading comprehension.

Questions and Activities to Build Background Knowledge:

1. Look at the front cover of the book and read the title. What do you think this book will be about?
2. What do you already know about this topic?
3. Take a book walk and skim the pages. Look at the table of contents, photographs, captions, and bold words. Did these text features give you any information or predictions about what you will read in this book?

Vocabulary: *Vocabulary Is Key to Reading Comprehension*

Use the following directions to prompt a conversation about each word.

- Read the vocabulary words.
- What comes to mind when you see each word?
- What do you think each word means?

Vocabulary Words:
- *bioluminescent*
- *camouflage*
- *invasive species*
- *sample bite*
- *toxic*
- *venomous*

During Reading: *Reading for Meaning and Understanding*

To achieve deep comprehension of a book, children are encouraged to use close reading strategies. During reading, it is important to have children stop and make connections. These connections result in deeper analysis and understanding of a book.

 Close Reading a Text

During reading, have children stop and talk about the following:

- Any confusing parts
- Any unknown words
- Text to text, text to self, text to world connections
- The main idea in each chapter or heading

Encourage children to use context clues to determine the meaning of any unknown words. These strategies will help children learn to analyze the text more thoroughly as they read.

When you are finished reading this book, turn to the next-to-last page for **After Reading Questions** and an **Activity.**

TABLE OF CONTENTS

WHAT MAKES A FISH DANGEROUS?

What do you imagine when you think of dangerous fish? You might think of scary teeth or sharp spikes. The facts may surprise you.

Some fish are dangerous. They can hurt animals or people. They can destroy plants. Others only seem dangerous.

SHARP SPINES AND ELECTRIC SHOCKS

Great white sharks are good hunters that can eat most ocean animals. They have many sharp teeth and can smell blood in the water. Some can smell one drop of blood in a million drops of water.

Would it surprise you to know that great white sharks only bite five to ten people a year? Most of the time, the curious shark takes a bite and swims away. This is called a **sample bite**.

Smile Big!

Great white sharks have 300 teeth. The teeth are in seven rows. Most people have only 32 teeth.

LOW   HIGH

DANGER METER

 sample bite (SAM-puhl bite): a bite that lets the animal taste something before eating it

Lionfish have sharp spikes on their backs. The spikes are **venomous**. Stepping on the spikes hurts, but it will not kill a person.

 venomous (VEN-uh-mus): able to hurt or kill with a poison by biting or stinging

invasive species (in-VAY-siv SPEE-sheez): a type of living thing that is brought into an environment and takes it over, causing harm

Lionfish are an **invasive species**. They eat many animals and have lots of young. Many other animals nearby cannot survive.

LOW HIGH

DANGER METER

Stonefish look like rocks. But they are the most venomous fish in the world. A person can die if they step on one.

Hide and Seek

Stonefish use **camouflage**. Can you find the stonefish on this page?

 camouflage (CAM-oh-flahj): a way to hide by blending into the background

LOW HIGH

DANGER METER

18

Electric eels can make electricity. If a human or other animal gets too close...ZAP! The shocks do not usually kill people, but they can kill small animals.

LOW HIGH

DANGER METER

Many parts of a pufferfish's body are **toxic**. Eating the liver, skin, or other parts can kill humans or other animals. The spikes on their bodies can hurt but are not deadly.

A Spiky Issue

Pufferfish got their name because they can puff up when threatened. They swallow water and make their bodies much larger.

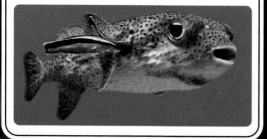

 toxic (TAHK-sik): dangerous if eaten

LOW HIGH

DANGER METER

MORE THAN SCARY STORIES

You might be scared if you met a huge whale shark in the ocean. But whale sharks only eat small animals and plants. They are harmless to people and most things in the water.

DANGER METER

LOW HIGH

Gentle Giant

Whale sharks are the biggest fish in the sea. They can grow as long as 40 feet (about 12 meters).

Anglerfish have large teeth and a **bioluminescent** light hanging from their forehead. They are good hunters. But they live far down in the dark ocean. Almost no people ever see them.

 bioluminescent (BYE-oh-loom-in-ess-ent): glowing because of chemicals in the body of a living thing

LOW HIGH

DANGER METER

LOW **HIGH**

DANGER METER

A piranha's sharp teeth can look dangerous. Their bites are powerful and can rip through flesh. But attacks on humans are rare and not deadly.

A Barking Fish?

Piranhas can make sounds when they are caught. Some sound like dogs barking.

Think about the fish around you. How are they like the animals in this book? How are they different? What do you think: Are they dangerous...or not?

LOW HIGH
DANGER METER

LOW HIGH
DANGER METER

LOW HIGH
DANGER METER

LOW HIGH
DANGER METER

MEMORY GAME

Look at the pictures. What do you remember reading on the pages where each image appeared?

INDEX

AFTER READING QUESTIONS

1. What are some ways that fish can be dangerous?
2. Do you think piranhas are very dangerous? Why or why not?
3. What does a whale shark eat?
4. What makes lionfish so dangerous?
5. Why is it important to be careful if you eat a pufferfish?

ACTIVITY

Pick one of the fish in this book. Imagine that you are teaching people about it. How dangerous is the fish? Decide how you would teach the people to stay safe around the fish. Act out what you would say.

ABOUT THE AUTHOR

Tracie Santos loves learning and writing about animals. She has worked in zoos and aquariums with some of the world's most dangerous animals. She lives in Columbus, Ohio, with her two hairless cats, who are not dangerous but look very strange.

www.rourkeeducationalmedia.com

PHOTO CREDITS: Cover, page 1: ©Media Production; pages 4-5: ©MediaProduction; pages 6-7: ©Vladimir Wrangel; pages 8-9, 30: ©Alessandro De Maddalena; pages 10-11: ©Stefan Pircher; pages 12-13, 30: ©momo11353; pages 14-15: ©Rich Carey; pages 16-17: ©izanbar; pages 18-19, 30: ©tristan tan; page 20 inset: ©Hans Gert Broeder; pages 20-21, 30: ©Beth Swanson; pages 22-23, 30: ©crisod; pages 24-25: ©panparinda; pages 26-27, 30: ©Jinny Jin; page 28a: ©MirekKijewski; page 28b: ©bbevren; page 29a: ©MattiaATH; page 29b: ©reisegraf; page 32: ©Taryn Lindsey

Edited by: Kim Thompson
Cover design by: Rhea Magaro-Wallace
Interior design by: Bobbie Houser

Library of Congress PCN Data

Sharks and Other Fish / Tracie Santos
(Dangerous...or Not?)
 ISBN 978-1-73163-818-2 (hard cover)
 ISBN 978-1-73163-895-3 (soft cover)
 ISBN 978-1-73163-972-1 (e-Book)
 ISBN 978-1-73164-049-9 (e-Pub)
Library of Congress Control Number: 2020930054

Rourke Educational Media
Printed in the United States of America
02-3262111937